Thank You for Being You

KAREN MOORE

Bristol Park Books

Bristol Park Books
252 West 38th Street
New York, NY 10018

First Bristol Park Books edition published in 2016

Bristol Park Books is a registered trademark
of Bristol Park Books, Inc.

Library of Congress Control Number: 2016936859

ISBN: 978-0-88486-620-6

E-Book ISBN: 978-0-88486-621-3

Text and cover design by Keira McGuinness
Cover and interior art copyright © 2016 Keira McGuinness

Printed in Malaysia

To

_____

From

_____

Introduction

This book is for those warm and wonderful people who make me laugh and inspire my gratitude. They walk beside me through thick and thin. They know when I'm at my best, or possibly even at my worst and they love me anyway. These are the people I choose to be with simply because they bring comfort when no one else can, and they make life feel okay again no matter what I face. I am grateful for authentic, loving friends; the amazing people who change my world for the better. They take on life, one smile and one tear at a time.

Thank you for being you!

—*Karen Moore*

Thank You for Being Kind

A kind heart is a fountain of gladness,
making everything in its vicinity
freshen with smiles.

—*Washington Irving*

You have a way of sowing seeds of kindness everywhere you go. You turn gravelly bits of dormant soil into blossoms of delight simply by your willingness to share your precious time, your gentle spirit, and your laughter. You also plant seeds of possibility and hope and you make a difference to everyone who knows you.

You can be sure that every kindness you offer ignites a light of joy in the hearts of your friends and family, causing them to want to choose to be a bit kinder themselves. You cast a vision that is sure and positive and one that fertilizes the soil of every relationship so that wonderful moments can flourish and withstand both the rain and sunshine of life.

St. Basil wrote, "The one who plants kindness, gathers love." May you continue to gather more love to share wherever you are and may your life benefit always from the kindness you show to others.

Where Kindness Walks

Follow kindness where it goes
And you'll soon notice that it grows
Everything with care.
When kindness walks into a room,
It quickly takes away the gloom
And puts its sunshine there.
Yes, kindness walks from place to place,
Bringing smiles to each face
For everyone to share.

If there is any kindness I can show,
Or any good thing I can do to anyone,
Let me do it now, and not deter or neglect it,
As I shall not pass this way again.
—*William Penn (adapted)*

What Possessed the Repo Man?

One of my favorite stories of kindness happened many years ago in a small upstate New York town. My Dad had just come back from serving in the army after the war was over. He and my mother were doing their best to get on their feet. They had two little children and an old house with leaky windows that allowed the winter breezes to come whistling through the kitchen.

One day, my dad was out looking for work in the nearby towns, driving their old rattle trap truck, hoping to find a supplement to the dwindling pay he was receiving from the army. While he was out, a man stopped by the house and knocked on the door. My mother answered with one baby on her hip and another in a high chair. The man asked to speak to my dad and since it was cold, my mother offered him a chair and a cup of coffee knowing my dad was due home any time.

The man looked around the house and noticed the plastic coverings to help keep the chill out of the room from the windows. He saw the old ironing board with the irons that had to be heated on the stove where my mom had been ironing. He looked around and made small talk.

My dad arrived soon after and chatted with the man for a bit. He knew the man had come to repossess his truck, but the man never said a word about it. Dad owed $300 on the truck and that was a lot of money. He couldn't pay it, and if he lost the truck, he couldn't find work very easily.

After finishing his coffee, the stranger stood, shook my dad's hand, and said, "I see you folks are working hard to keep things together here."

Dad said yes, and that he was trying to find a job. He knew he owed money on the truck, but it was his only way to look for work. The man wished them well and left. About two weeks later Dad got a letter in the mail. It said that the truck was now paid in full.

That stranger had compassion and kindness for my parents. Soon Dad found a job so he could keep his family fed and housed. Kindness made a difference.

A Dance of Kindness

People often pass us by
Weighed down by circumstance,
And though we vaguely see them
We hardly share a glance.
But then a voice within us
Says take a little chance,
And with a word, or just a smile
We join the kindness dance.

Never lose a chance of saying a kind word.
—*William Makepeace Thackeray*

Friends. . . they cherish one another's hopes.
They are kind to one another's dreams.
—*Henry David Thoreau*

Thank You
for Being a
Loving Person

When love is the focus of our work, every day
is payday.

—Anonymous

You approach the world heart first. You look for the good in any situation and you give credit to people beyond what they generally deserve. You define love with a smile and a warm hello. How do you do this? You do it by having genuine concern for the feelings of other people. You honor them for who they are and you respect their circumstances. You never try too hard to get them to hear your opinion or accept your ideas. You simply love them as they are.

You offer guidance when someone asks for it and you always seek to listen as much as you talk. You're an amazing and loving listener.

Thank you for being someone that causes others to want to be more generous. Your love is a gift that flows from your heart and those around you appreciate it. You are such an inspiration!

Be present when you meet others face to face;
share your heart, accepting and acknowledging
those who draw near you with love.
For true love is inexhaustible; the more you
give, the more you have.

—Antoine De Saint Exupery

You will find as you look back upon your life,
that the moments when you really lived are the
moments when you have done things in the
spirit of love.

—Henry Drummond

Love is the fulfillment of all our works. There is
the goal; that is why we run: we run toward it,
and once we reach it, in it we shall find rest.

—Augustine of Hippo

Love Stories

Most of us grew up with soap operas on TV which were probably nothing like real, good love stories. But your story of love isn't a weekly TV episode. Your story is about the way you love your friends. Your love story is about your family and the interactions and exchanges that help you grow together and face the challenges life brings. Your love story means when you walk in the door every person that draws near you gets to take a little of your love supply home with them. It's an amazing story.

You will have endless love stories to tell because you create those stories with each relationship. You treat people in loving ways; you expect the best of others; people who know you try to give you their best in return.

Your love stories take you through storms and stony ground, but you never give up on the possibility for love to win. Thank you for bringing your love gifts to every situation.

Beyond the Soaps

In TV soaps,
Each episode
Sets love in motion
To explode.
It winds us up
And spits us out
Shaken, taken up
With doubt.
But thankfully
We don't conceal
The kind of love
We know is real,
For we're beyond
The lagging hopes

Of washed-up stories
On the soaps.
So if you spend
A time or two

Wondering if
The soaps are true,
Don't spend a moment
Being vexed
Just send a simple
Little text,
And I'll remind you
Love's a blend
Of all we share
Friend to friend!

Thank You for Being Very Thoughtful

houghtful people rarely recognize the gift they are to others. They simply do the kindest things in the nicest ways because it is their nature to do so. They not only acknowledge others, but they genuinely care about them. They make a difference with each opportunity to offer kindness and thoughtful deeds.

You're the one who shows up when others leave; the one who looks for the best in a situation; one who thinks before you speak. You respect the thoughts of others and you make each person in your midst feel important.

You're thoughtful in ways that few people are. Your smile welcomes friends and strangers alike. You have so many ways of being kind that it's even hard to list them all, but for each one you deserve thanks.

Thoughtless and Thoughtful

Thoughtless and *Thoughtful*
Are equal life-changers,
One inspires real friendships,
One bumps into strangers.
Thoughtful would help
A person in need
Thoughtless would cringe
And reverse
The good deed.
Thoughtful would try
To even the score,
By being more kind
Than she was before.
Then *Thoughtless*
Would answer with a glare,
"You can't win the world
It's so thoughtless out there.

You'll never be able
To go out there and fix
The thoughtless world
With your kindly tricks.
It just won't work,
You can't ever win,"
Said *Thoughtless* proudly
With a wide-open grin.
Then *Thoughtful* replied,
"Here's what I'll do,
I won't change the world,
I'll simply change you."
And it didn't take long,
Perhaps you've already heard,
Thoughtless was changed—by one thoughtful word!

You Are Thoughtful When...

You remember special occasions

You encourage my thinking

You honor who I am as a person

You laugh with me about little things

You love me just as I am

You think before you speak

You know when to ask questions and when to be silent

You stick with me through thick and thin

You offer positive ideas

You lighten my load

Thank You
for Listening

You're a Great Listener

You form your thoughts so quietly,
With words that simply glisten,
And so you're loved by all your friends
For the loving ways you listen.

You Listen to My Heart

You have a way of listening that calms my inner-most being, my spirit. You don't just listen for words, but you listen for real understanding. You take in body language and facial expressions. In a word, you listen with your heart.

It's a gift to be a good listener, to not be distracted by your own concerns, but to be able to listen intently, with focused interest to someone else. Most of us are easily drawn off by cell phones ringing and endless little interruptions. We listen, much of the time, with half an ear.

Thank you for being a listening friend. You open the door for warm communication and sharing heart to heart. You inspire new thinking and quiet assurance. You hear with both ears and take genuine interest in the well-being of someone else.

> We have two ears and one mouth so that we can listen twice as much as we speak.
> —*Epictetus*

> Be quick to listen, slow to speak, and slow to get angry.
>
> —*James 1:19, (NLT)*

Listening with Love

Some people talk
And some people hear,
But few people listen
And draw others near.

The talkers are thinking
About what else to say
And the listeners are anxious
To get on their way.

They stay on the surface,
"How are you? Please call!"
Then go on their way
Hearing nothing at all.

No conversation
Really took place,
For neither one listened
With love or with grace.

Yet, people like you
Focus right from the start,
Taking in every word
With a listening heart.

Thanks for Being There

Thanks for Being There

It's 3 A.M. My head is full of stories and my mind won't quiet down. I've tried counting sheep and drinking warm milk and listening to soothing water sounds, but nothing is working. The only thing that feels like it might possibly help is to make a phone call to my dearest friend, the person who knows you like no one else does and who will be able to hear your heart and calm your fears.

I know it's late, but I simply must talk to someone. I ring that familiar phone number and a sleepy voice answers. I explain what is going on and my friend comes to life, ready to listen, with no need for apology for the hour.

You are the friend who is there when needed. It doesn't matter what time of day or night it is, or where you are, you make yourself available and let compassion be your guide. You make me feel so grateful, grateful to know you, and grateful to call you a beloved friend.

My Three A.M. Friend

The late night shows
Are out of talk,
It's much too late
To take a walk
And yet I'm up
Still wide awake,
I read a book,
I tried to bake,
But nothing stops
My noisy head
From spinning tales
That cause me dread.

It's 3. A. M.
What can I do?
I find my cell

And I call you.
Your voice just soothes me
Instantly.
As you connect to me
At 3.

You ask if I'm all right,
Okay,
And what has happened
In my day?

It isn't long
Before the noise
Subsides and brings me
Needed joys,
Because you are
My friend indeed
And always answer
Any need.

So thanks, my Friend,
For being you
And loving me
The way you do.
Thanks for being
There for me
At any time,
Even 3!

Being There at the Right Time

*A*nna was a manager in a small manufacturing business. A new associate had been working for her for only a couple days asked if she could speak with Anna privately. Behind closed doors, the new employee, Jane, revealed that she was going through difficult things in her personal life and that she was not sure what her direction should be. She feared that her husband was preparing to leave her and so she took a job out of desperation, knowing she would need it to support their children.

Anna listened intently to the story and asked Jane what she wanted to do. She said she was sorry to hear of such a stressful situation and if Jane needed a couple days to reflect on all this, she was welcome to take time off, with no dock in pay, and then come back to work and let Anna know how she'd like to move forward.

Jane left. She returned two days later. She told Anna that now she was ready to work hard at her new job. And Jane did. Eventually, Jane reconciled with her husband, but had to leave the company because he was being transferred to a different state and they were working hard to strengthen their marriage. Jane and Anna parted amicably.

Several years later, Jane and Anna met each other again, quite by accident.

"I don't think you know what you did for me all those years ago." Jane said.

Anna smiled and said that she was pleased that things had worked out.

Jane took her hand and said, "No, you don't understand. You saved my life. I was going to kill myself right after work that day. Your willingness to listen, and help me when I was in the greatest need, made all the difference. You were my angel."

Anna realized that she had somehow done the right thing at the right time, even though she never imagined the extent of the pain Jane was going through. But she was there for Jane when she was most needed. You are that kind of friend.

Thank You
for Making
A Difference

Making A Difference

You may not always know it,
Or even be aware,
Of how you make a difference
Just by being there.

You always know just what to say
When everything is crazy
And you bring out all the sunshine
When my thoughts are gray and hazy.

You really make a difference
Just by being you
And my heart is filled with gratitude
For all the things you do.

Sometimes our light goes out but is blown into flame by another human being. Each of us owes deepest thanks to those who have rekindled this light.

—Albert Schweitzer

Our critical day is not the very day of our death, but the whole course of our life; I thank them that pray for me when my bell tolls; but I thank them much more, that catechize me, or preach to me, or instruct me how to live.

—John Donne

To ease another's heartache is to forget one's own.

—Abraham Lincoln

Thank You for Being Charitable

You're a giver! You can't help yourself. Wherever you see a need, wherever you can lend a hand, if you have time and resources, you're there. Sometimes charity is equated with the word "love." You're a person who loves others in big ways and you're generous with everything you have. Know that you are an example to me.

With your loving guidance, I often find myself wondering how to be more charitable myself. I have heard that charity begins at home so that makes me think of my family and friends first, the people that are nearest and dearest to me.

But I know that you open your heart and mind to the world and embrace it. You just do it. You keep making the effort, offering your best at any time for all.

Charity is twice blessed—it blesses the one
who gives and the one who receives.

—Author unknown

Charity should begin at home,
but should not stay there.

—Philip Brooks

Even if it's a little thing, do something for those
who have need of help, something for which you
get no pay but the privilege of doing it.

—Albert Schweitzer

You Always "Pay It Forward."

Some folks are on the waiting list,
They wait and wait and wait.
They wait for others to show love
And rid the world of hate.

They huff and puff and holler
Because things never change
And yet they never notice
They have something to exchange.

For any of us, any time
Can be the ones who strive
To fix the messes that we see
And keep real love alive.

And you're that kind of person,
The one who shines a light
On those you find in need
And you help to make things right.

You offer them a helping hand,
And "pay it forward" as they say,
Because you know that only you
Can brighten up their day.

So thank you for the attitude
Of giving from your heart
To friends and even strangers
Where you always do your part.

A Good Samaritan

Some people have the hearts of true Samaritans. Like the story in the Bible about a man who sees a victim of a crime, lying in a ditch on the side of the road. He stops and offers help and pays for the victim's needs. True Samaritans don't ask for something in exchange. They don't ask for a "thank you" note to be delivered to their door. They simply give, because giving is what they do. They know that being part of the solution is the only way to help balance the scales in a world of problems. Thank you for all you do with a Good Samaritan's heart!

Something to Remember

One simple rule,

To remember yet

Is that human beings

Are in each other's debt.

And the more we give

Of love and care

The more we'll have

That we can share.

Thank You
for Being So
Much Fun

Hearty laughter is a good way to jog internally without having to go outdoors.

—Norman Cousins

You're the kind of friend who makes a room feel brighter and merrier just because you walked into it. You bring out the laughter and the sparkle that everyone needs, especially me. It's hard to imagine what the world would be like if there weren't people who made others stop for a moment, take a break from their seriousness, and realize that life is meant to be enjoyed.

Thank you for being that kind of person to everyone who knows you. You contribute to our better nature and make us want to be kinder and warmer and even a bit sillier.

Laugh with Me

Nothing works its magic
Like laughter and a friend
Clouds break up and float away
And drift around the bend.
All the frets and worries
Whirling round my head,
Are lost in laughter's merriment
And bring sweet joy instead.

Yes, it simply is amazing
How laughter finds a way
Of changing gloomy troubles
Into a brighter day.

So come along, my friend
And let's be light and free
Leave all our cares behind—
Yes, come and laugh with me!

You Put a Smile on My Face

You put a smile on my face
That time will surely not erase,
You're positive and sweet and funny,
And keep things light and bright and sunny,
You make me laugh when we're together
No matter what the wind or weather,
It's certain that my whole life through
I'll smile each time I think of you!

A sense of humor...is needed armor. Joy in
one's heart and some laughter on one's lips is
a sign that the person down deep has a pretty
good grasp of life.

—Hugh Sidney

Friends have lots of reasons to laugh out loud together. After all, they know each other's secrets and they've been through the tough times and the tender ones and they're still going strong. They can laugh when you spill your iced tea all over the table and everyone else, or when you leave that toilet tissue hanging out of your shoe as you emerge from the restroom at your favorite lunch spot. Almost anything at all can trigger an endless stream of teary-eyed laughter.

There's nothing like a friend with a great sense of humor. You make everyone glad to be around you. I am grateful that you are just the way you are…warm, funny, and full of joy.

Thank You
for Sharing
Your Talents

Friends come in a variety of shapes and sizes. The best ones help shape my life in ways that give it greater dimension. They encourage me to grow and become more than I might ever have been without them. They have an array of skills and talents and they make my world more interesting just by what they share.

I love learning from you. You open up my world to think a little differently and to try something I would never attempt without you to guide me. You give me a chance to gain a new perspective and open up the windows and doors of my thinking so that a blast of fresh air can come in.

Oh, the Things You Can Do!
(with apologies to Dr. Seuss)

Oh, the things you can do
When you set your mind to it,
It's amazing to me just to see
How you do it.
You can pick out a present
And wrap it just right
Tied with stringers and streamers
And things that delight.
You can cheer up a neighbor
Or a friend in the dumps,
And you do it with kindness
With no thumps, blips, or bumps.
You're one talented woman
There's no doubt about it,
Why everyone everywhere
Is ready to shout it.
You work with your hands

And make magical dishes
From soups to nut sauces
Or sautéed salmon fishes.
It's great to partake
Of the things you can do
For there's nobody out there
With more talent than you.
It's a wonder a thunder
Of claps and applause
And shouts of hooray
And the sweetest guffaws,
Don't follow you everywhere,
You might happen to go,
Because you're a woman of wonder
That it's awesome to know!
So thanks for the sharing
Of your nimble nice ways
And for lifting and gifting us
All of our days!

Use your gifts faithfully,
And they shall be enlarged;
Practice what you know,
And you shall attain to higher knowledge.
                                    —*Matthew Arnold*

Neither a lofty degree of intelligence nor
imagination nor both together go to the
making of genius. Love, love, love, that is
the soul of genius.

                    —*Mozart*

You don't hide your talents under a bushel. You share them so we can enjoy them all. You give us hope about what we might do and stimulate us to try harder.

Thank You for Your Generous Hospitality

You have a way of welcoming people into your heart as well as into your home. You don't just show us your kitchen, you bake a pie. You treat everyone with such kindness and love that we feel like we've known you forever. It's a gift that few people have and so I'm so grateful every time you open the door of welcome to me.

Some people let you stand in the hallway of their lives, but never let you enter any further. Others might invite you into the dining room for a nice meal, but they'd never let you into the kitchen. You're a master at letting people into your life. You never make anyone feel like they are a stranger to you; on the outside looking in.

It's been said that all of us should welcome strangers, because it's possible that we might be entertaining angels and not even know it. You are a hospitality angel.

The Welcome Mat

"Hello, come on in,

How nice to see you here,

Sure glad you found the time

To visit me and bring some cheer.

Let's talk out on the porch swing,

And I'll make some unsweet tea

And I'll bring some sugar cookies

That I baked for you and me.

The welcome mat is always out

I love the doorbell chime,

For nothing fills me with delight

Like a little friendship time."

Spread love everywhere you go: First of all in your own house...let no one ever come to you without leaving better and happier.

—Mother Teresa

What do we live for if it is not to make life less difficult for each other?

—George Eliot

The glory of friendship is not the
    outstretched hand,
nor the kindly smile, nor the joy
    of companionship;
it is the spiritual inspiration that comes to one
    when he discovers that
someone else believes in him and is willing to
    trust him with his friendship.

— Waldo Emerson

You can never establish a personal relationship
without opening up your own heart.
—*Paul Tournier*

You Welcome Me with Open Arms

Your arms of friendship welcome me

And gladly take me in,

You're there for me with kindness—

A friend through thick and thin.

There's no one quite like you

And your loving, gentle heart,

It's good to know you're always there

Even when we're miles apart.

Thank You
for Being
With
Me Through
Tough Times

hank you for being the friend who will talk me off the ledges and get me turned around so that I can think straight again; and the one who will celebrate with me for the good things in life. I don't know what I would do without you.

You are the friend who is willing to stick with me in the tough times; does not expect anything from me, or want something in return for your generosity.

You are my go-to person. I think of you immediately when trouble rears its ugly face. You remind me that friends, real friends stick together no matter what happens. There's a kind of contentment in knowing that I'd be okay if any crisis hit me, because I would have you to turn to; to help me get through it.

The Tough Times Friend

When the weeds are growing taller
And the sunlight starts to fade,
The first thing some folks notice
Is the big ole mess you've made.
They wait to see just what you'll do
And send a greeting card or letter—
They say they hope you're fine now
And that everything is better.
The trouble is that trouble
Doesn't bring a special hoe
To weed out all the obstacles
Where brand new seeds can grow.
And trouble won't apologize
Or fix things in a hurry,
In fact it steals your choices
And leaves you just to worry.
But real friends walk right to your door,
And bravely ring the bell

With a bag of needed groceries
And some apple pie as well.
They fill your heart with laughter
And they listen to you too,
And then they put their hand in yours
And ask, "What can I do?"
And that's how good friends manage
To plant joy where worry grew
And how they help to quickly fix
The things that bothered you.
And once the mess is over,
They remind you in the end
That nothing means as much to them
As being your good friend.

A real friend walks into your life, when the rest
of the world walks out.

—*Walter Winchell*

As aromatic plans bestow
No spicy fragrance while they grow,
But crushed or trodden to the ground,
Diffuse their balmy sweets around.

—Oliver Goldsmith

The good things which belong to prosperity are
    to be wished,
But the good things that belong to adversity are
    to be admired.

—Seneca

True friendship is a plant of low growth,
and must undergo and withstand the shocks of
    adversity
before it is entitled to the appellation.

—George Washington

There is no wilderness like a life without
   friends;
Friendship multiplies blessings and minimizes
   misfortunes;
It is a unique remedy against adversity, and it
   soothes the soul.

                              —*Baltasar Gracian*

***There will seldom be a friend like you**, who sees me*
just as I am and loves me anyway. You walk with me through the
hard times and you laugh with me through the better times. You
pull me together when I fall apart and shake me up when I need
to think about something again or gain a new perspective.

   You are always there for me with an open heart and a helping
hand for anything I might need.

Thank You for Being an Optimist

You always see the sunny side of things, the possibilities in the rocky events that might throw others off the track. You see new experiences as learning opportunities and ways to move forward. You have a positive perspective when my heart is sinking into the gloom.

When I can't see the good things all around me, or when I've become so focused on one difficulty that I can't see anything else in a positive way, you always pull me out of the mucky stuff and help me get back on my feet.

You have an amazing influence on my thinking and remind me to look for the joy in whatever I have to do.

The Secret to a Happy Life

It turns out when you meet someone
You have a choice to make,
To either be most pleasant
Or be one who's hard to take,
You set the tone for talking
With your smile and your greeting
And make someone feel glad or not
You had the chance of meeting.
It seems like something simple,
No big secret, nothing to it,
Anyone and everyone
Can take the time to do it.
It's all about your attitude
And the peaceful light you bring
That really makes you happy
In the midst of everything.
So, there really is no secret,
Nothing here that is brand new,
The key is treating others
As you hope they will treat you!

You grew up with the golden rule. You know that most people respond warmly to a smile, a wish for a great day, or a helping hand. You do those things without even thinking because it's such an important part of your DNA; it's how you are wired.

When the heart weeps for what it has lost, the spirit laughs for what it has found.

—Author unknown

A pessimist sees the difficulty in every opportunity; an optimist sees the opportunity in every difficulty.

—Winston Churchill

The optimist thinks this is the best that could ever be, and the pessimist knows it.

—J. Robert Oppenheimer

All things are possible to one who believes, yet more to one who hopes, more still to one who loves, and most of all to one who practices and perseveres in these three virtues.

—Brother Lawrence

"If a man does not keep pace with his companions, perhaps it is because he hears a different drummer. Let him step to the music which he hears, however measured or far away."

—Henry David Thoreau

If You Should Miss Plan "A"

The thing you do so well,
That brightens up my day,
Is knowing that you never fret
If you should miss plan **A.**

You simply grin and try again
And usher in Plan **B,**
And if that doesn't work so well,
You'll open up plan **C.**

It's amazing just to watch you
As you work each special plan
And it's awesome that you never think
That you've done all you can.

You go to **D** and **E** and **F**
With grace and great aplomb,
Knowing that you still have **G**

And **H** and **I** to come.

You look up high into the sky
And **J** and **K** are there,
You know that everything is fine
With **L** and **M** to spare.

You've got your plans all moving now
To **N** and **O** and **P**,
And even if they fail to rise
There's more that you can see.

You'll just try **Q** and **R** and **S**
And with inspired flash,
You'll pull up plans **T** and **U**
And make a steady dash,

To **V** and **W** and **X**
And whatever else you need,
And since you never hesitate,

Your plans go on full speed.

And even if you get to **Y**
Or all the way to **Z,**
Then you just say, "Oh, lucky day!
What joy this brings to me!"

You always have a brand new plan,
Because you know it's true,
That if your plans just go awry,
Then you can count on YOU!

You're such an inspiration,
Because for you, it's clear
That should you miss plan **A,**
Your next plan will appear!

Thanks
for
Being
A
Beautiful
Example

You're an example of patience and cheerfulness
and spontaneity. These are attributes that others only wish they
had. You always remind me that a little common sense and a
little compassion can make all the difference to your friends and
neighbors. You are a good person to follow.

Your friends follow your example because they appreciate you
so much. You're a wonderful example of what it means to be a
loving human being, a good friend, and a gentle presence in the
world. You are a born leader.

If there's a grown-up version of "Follow the Leader," then
I'm happy to get in line behind you.

> In everything set an example
> by doing what is good.
> —*Titus 2:7 (KJV)*

You're like a dance teacher. You do amazing and awesome things and others try to follow in your footsteps. Those around you follow your way of giving a welcome smile or the way you let life roll along without having to always determine its direction.

You make these things look easy, but they are really hard. At least, they are for me, but I know it's worth trying because you lead the way with such grace and beauty. It's a joy to walk in the footsteps of people I care about, or at least to walk alongside them on the same path.

> Setting an example is not the main means of influencing others, it is the only means.
> —*Albert Einstein*

Getting In Step

Step up,

Step back,

Step around, if you please.

Step over

Step under

Step along with ease!

Step to it,

Step on it,

Step aside for now,

Step ahead,

Step it up

Step by step, that's how.

Thank You
for Your
Forgiving Heart

You are forgiving. You know that nothing is more important than the present; nothing can be done about a moment in the past. You know that today we all can start again and make a difference.

You know how to forgive, not just in words, but from the heart. You forgive yourself and the actions of others. They are not meant to be carried around like excess baggage from place to place.

> Forgiveness is not an occasional act,
>   it is an attitude.
>   —*Martin Luther King, Jr.*

> To carry a grudge is like being stung to death by one bee.
>   —*William H. Walton*

The quality of mercy is not strain'd,
It droppeth as the gentle rain from heaven
Upon the place beneath; it is twice blest;
It blesses him that gives, and him that takes.
                        —*William Shakespeare*

Try Some Sweet Forgiveness Glue

Perhaps we need forgiveness glue
When things are torn apart,
Or when we're holding shreds of friendship
That's a matter of the heart.

Sometimes we need to start again,
To let the winds of change,
Blow away the dust and strain
Of things we can't exchange.

Friends like you are what we need,
The ones who sort things through
And help us to feel whole again
With sweet forgiveness glue.

You know just how to patch things up,
And when it's said and done,
You're ready once again to share
Life's craziness and fun.

So thanks for being willing
To repair and help renew
Our friendship when it's messy
With your sweet forgiveness glue.

Thank You
for Caring

You support my ups and downs and my successes and my failures. When my dreams manage to tank all at once, you help me step back and look at the rubble and try again to put the pieces together. Pebble by pebble, bit by bit, things take shape again and your caring attitude makes all the difference.

I don't always recognize success. But you have a way of making me feel that the effort itself is a form of success. Thanks to your friendship and caring heart, I have begun to see myself in more positive ways. You help to bring out the best of me.

I keep learning from you that it's okay to fall down, as long as I pick myself up and look for a new path. Your help and support challenges me to believe, trust and try again.

You're a Support Group of One

There are lots of big support groups,
For the losses we all bear,
Some facilitate recovery
Through stories that they share.

Some offer gentle guidance
For the days that will yet be
And some remind the spirit
That it's good to be set free.

But you are something special,
A support group all in one,
And you probably don't realize
The many things you've done.

You support me as a friend,
Encouraging my heart,
Giving me ideas

When I don't know where to start.
You laugh at all my stories,
Telling stories of your own,
And you show up in those moments
When I'm feeling all alone.

You have a way of caring
That few can ever boast,
And I would raise my glass to you
If we should make a toast.

You help me see the difference
Between failure and success
And shine a light on all it means
To share real happiness.

You are a support group,
That is second to none,
Because you're simply the best of them
Rolled right into one!

I've learned from our friendship that the more I keep myself in balance, the more I realize my own strengths and weaknesses and the more I strive to become the best possible me, the more I can be a good friend.

> True happiness…arises, in the first place, from
> the enjoyment of one's self, and, in the next,
> from friendship and conversation of a few
> selected companions.
> —*Joseph Addison*

The Friendship Box

Let's create a friendship box
Where the walls will intersect
With the strength of things we value
Like love and great respect.

Let's fill the box with moments
We'll recall when we're apart,
Those times we helped each other
In the matters of the heart.

Let's add some bits of sympathy,
Courtesy and pride,
And hold each message closely
That we have tucked inside.

Yes, let's create a friendship box,
That's just for you and me
And the memories and dreams we've known
And things still yet to be.

For there's nothing quite like friendship
To bring true happiness
And your friendship means far more to me
Than you might ever guess!

It's not just anyone who can give advice with love the way that you so often do. You have a way of helping me take another look at different ways I might think or act. You shine a light that gives me room to grow and try again.

Thank You
for Your
Encouragement

You're the friend who makes it easy for me to ask for an opinion; you give your advice with love and thoughtfulness. You make it easy to share what's going on; no need for pretense or concern about being vulnerable. You know, there are not many people like you; ones who can be trusted with another person's worries and fears.

Your willingness to share your thoughts about important matters makes you an irresistible friend, one that creates a stronghold in the shaky moments life brings.

Saying the right word at the right time
is so pleasing.

—Proverbs 15:23, (NCV)

By three methods we may learn wisdom:
First, by reflection, which is noblest;
Second, by imitation, which is easiest; and
Third by experience, which is the bitterest.

—Confucius

A true friend unbosoms freely, advises justly,
assists readily, adventures boldly, takes all
patiently, defends courageously, and continues
a friend unchangeably.

—William Penn

A Little Bit of Wisdom;
a Whole Lot of Love

Whether you are sharing
Some sage advice and wit,
Or whether you are speaking words
For each one's benefit,
You always seem to know just what to say.
You offer bits of wisdom
With a smile in your eyes
And a courage in your heart
That makes others realize
That better things are sure to come their way.
Thanks for all your kind advice
So gently given, we don't mind it,
Because we know with certainty
All the love you put behind it—
Love that brings a blessing to a day.

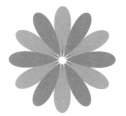

Thank
You
for
Being
You!

You

You cheer me on and keep me going,
And hold me tight when winds are blowing.
Your kindness keeps me standing tall
You pick me up each time I fall,
You laugh a lot and cry some too,
We're lucky to have me and you.
You help me triumph over things
And in a pinch, you give me wings,
You're there with every rising tide,
Sticking closely to my side.
You're a great companion and a friend,
And we'll be stuck until the end
For we're the glue that holds us tight
And helps to set the whole world right.
We're more than family, as you know,
And loved much more than words can show,
So please remember, 'cause it's true,
We're so lucky to have me and you.

You are a friend in all the best ways. You're there when help is needed and you chip in cheerfully to make sure all the right things get done. You're like family to me. We may not have grown up together, but we're definitely growing as we help each other negotiate our days and navigate the world.

Walking with a friend in the dark is better than walking alone in the light.

—Helen Keller

True friendship multiplies the good in life and divides its evils. Strive to have friends, for life without friends is like life on a desert island…to find one real friend in a lifetime is good fortune; to keep him is a blessing.

—Baltasar Gracian

> It is one of the blessings of old friends that you
> can afford to be stupid with them.
> —*Ralph Waldo Emerson*

What more could a person hope for in any kind of relationship, but to truly be understood, to strive to understand, to take life one day at a time; and to have one moment, one special heartfelt chat at any time at all. You will always make the people around you grateful that you arrived on this planet to walk beside them. After all, there's really no one else quite like you.

Thank you for being you!